The Easter Story

Published by Candle Books
an imprint of
Lion Hudson plc
Wilkinson House, Jordan Hill Road,
Oxford OX2 8DR, England
www.lionhudson.com/candle

ISBN 978 1 78128 177 2
e-ISBN 978 1 78128 189 5

First edition 2015

A catalogue record for this book is available
from the British Library

Printed and bound in China,
October 2014, LH06

The Easter Story

BY JULIET DAVID
ILLUSTRATED BY ELINA ELLIS

CANDLE BOOKS

Jesus goes to Jerusalem

Jesus healed lots of sick people and did wonderful miracles. He told great stories. He was the friend of many.

There was an important festival called Passover in Jerusalem. Jesus decided to go with his special friends, the twelve disciples.

On their way to Jerusalem Jesus said,
"I'm going to be arrested and killed.
But after three days, I will be raised from the dead."
His friends didn't understand what he meant.

Jesus borrows a donkey

When they arrived near a village called Bethany,
Jesus sent off two of his friends.

"Go to the next village," he told them.
"There you'll find a donkey. Nobody has ever ridden it.
Untie that donkey and bring it to me.
If anyone asks what you're doing, just say,
'Our master needs the donkey!'"

The two disciples found the donkey, as Jesus had said
they would. They untied it and brought it to Jesus.

Then some of Jesus' friends spread their cloaks
over the donkey's back.

Hooray for God!

Jesus climbed on the borrowed donkey and rode into Jerusalem.

Lots of people were going into the city for the festival.

When the crowds saw Jesus coming, they grew very excited.

Some people spread their cloaks on the ground before Jesus.

Others cut down branches from palm trees and laid them on the road.

Soon almost everyone was shouting,

"Hosanna! Hooray for God!"

9

Priests plot against Jesus

Some of the priests from the Temple hated Jesus.
They were plotting to kill him.

One of Jesus' disciples, Judas Iscariot, met with the chief priests.

"If you pay me," said Judas, "I will show you
where you can find Jesus – and arrest him."

The priests were delighted.

They promised Judas thirty silver coins for doing this.

Judas waited for a good time to hand Jesus over to them.

Jesus cleans up the Temple

When he arrived in Jerusalem, Jesus went to visit the Temple.

Lots of shopkeepers had set up tables there.

They were selling things and changing money.

Jesus was very angry.

"You've made God's Temple into a robbers' den!" he shouted.

Then Jesus chased these men right out of the Temple.

He pushed over their tables and stalls.

"God's Temple should be a place of prayer
for all the nations of the world," said Jesus.

A very special meal

The day arrived for the feast of Passover.

Jesus wanted to eat this meal with his twelve disciples. He met with them in an upstairs room in Jerusalem.

Before they ate, Jesus took off his coat and poured water into a bowl.
Then he started to wash his disciples' feet.

He wanted to show his friends that they should care for each other,
just as he cared for them.

Then all twelve disciples sat down with Jesus to eat supper.

Bread and wine

As they ate together, Jesus said, "Love one another, as I love you."
Later he said, "One of you eating this meal with me
is going to hand me over to my enemies."

The disciples looked
very worried.

"It's the person who
is eating from the same
bowl as me," said Jesus.

"Surely you can't mean
me, Master?" said Judas.

"Yes, it is you," said Jesus.

Just then Judas crept out.

He was plotting against Jesus.

Jesus took some bread. He thanked God for it, broke it,
and gave some to each of his friends.

Then Jesus took a cup of wine.
He thanked God for it and passed it to his disciples.

After the meal, they all sang a hymn.

Jesus prays alone

As night fell, Jesus took his disciples to a garden outside the city.

"Wait here!" he said. "I want to pray alone. Stay awake – and pray too!"

Then Jesus took three special friends a bit further with him
– Peter, James, and John.

"Stay here and pray," he asked them.

Jesus went a little further still and prayed on his own.

Jesus came back to find his three friends.
They were all fast asleep!
"Peter!" Jesus said, waking him. "Why are you sleeping?
Couldn't you pray for just an hour?"
Then Jesus went back to the garden to pray.
But the disciples soon fell asleep again.

Judas kisses Jesus

A little later, Jesus came back.
"Wake up!" he said. "Here comes
the man who is going to hand me
over to my enemies!"
Judas was leading men
carrying swords and sticks.
"The man I kiss is
the one you must arrest,"
Judas told the priests.
Judas walked up to Jesus,
kissed him, and said, "Teacher!"
Then the soldiers with Judas
knew this was Jesus.
They grabbed him
and took him prisoner.
The disciples were scared.
They all ran off
and left Jesus alone.

To the cross!

The soldiers marched Jesus off to be judged.

"Are you the Son of God?" asked the high priest.

"Yes!" Jesus answered.

"Did you hear?" the priests shouted angrily.
"He says he's the Son of God!"

Next day the priests took Jesus to the Roman ruler, Pilate.

"This man Jesus is making a lot of trouble," they told him.
"You *must* put him to death!"

"I can find nothing wrong with him," said Pilate.
Then he turned to the crowd who were watching.
"What shall I do with Jesus?" asked Pilate.
The crowd all shouted, "Put him on a cross!"
"Then I will send him to die," said Pilate.

A lonely hill

Now cruel Roman soldiers started making fun of Jesus.
  They mocked him and pretended to salute him.
  Finally the soldiers marched Jesus to a hill outside the city.
There they fixed him on a wooden cross.

They also put two robbers on crosses, one on each side of Jesus.
At midday the sky suddenly went dark.
Three hours later, Jesus died.
A Roman captain said, "This really *was* God's Son!"
Jesus' family and some of his friends stood watching sadly.

Jesus is buried

After Jesus had died, a good man named Joseph went to Pilate.

"Jesus is dead," he said. "May I look after his body?"

Pilate nodded, "Yes, you may!"

So Joseph took Jesus' body from the cross. He wrapped it in a cloth and laid it in a grave carved out of rock.

Finally Joseph rolled a huge stone across the doorway of the grave, so that Jesus' body wouldn't be disturbed.

Two Roman soldiers stood guard at the door.

An empty tomb!

Early on Sunday morning, Jesus' friend Mary Magdalene went to his tomb.

She took some perfume to put on his body.

When she arrived, Mary was astonished to see that the big stone in front of the door had been rolled back. And she couldn't see Jesus' body anywhere.

Mary dashed off back to Jerusalem.

She wanted to tell Peter and John what she had just seen.

"They've taken away Jesus' body!" she cried. "I couldn't find it!"

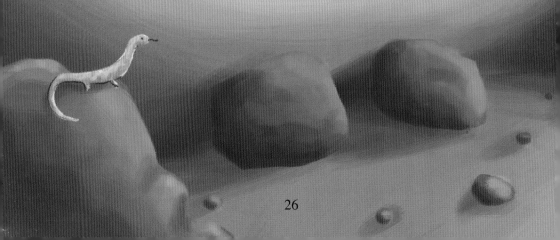

27

Race to the tomb

Peter and John decided to look for themselves.
They both rushed off to Jesus' tomb.
John arrived first; he was younger
and ran faster than Peter.
As soon as he arrived,
John bent down and peered inside.
Then Peter ran up, almost
out of breath. He dashed
straight into the tomb.
The sheets that Jesus had
been wrapped in were
neatly folded up.

But there was no body.

Suddenly an angel appeared.

"Jesus isn't here," said the angel.
"He's alive!"

Immediately Peter and John believed
that Jesus had risen from the dead.

Jesus appears to Mary

Peter and John hurried back into Jerusalem.

But Mary Magdalene stayed outside the tomb, crying. She peered into the tomb again.

Now Mary saw two angels.

"Why are you crying?" they asked her.

"They've taken Jesus' body away," Mary answered. "I don't know *where* to find it."

Mary turned and saw Jesus standing there – but she didn't recognize him.

"Why are you crying?" he asked her. "Who are you looking for?"

Mary thought he was the gardener.

"If you've taken Jesus' body," she said, "*please* tell me where you've put it!"

Jesus just said, "Mary!"

At once she knew it was Jesus.

"Teacher!" she said.

Mary rushed off to find the disciples.

"I've seen Jesus," she told them. "He's alive!"

31

Jesus meets two friends

After Jesus died, two of his followers were walking to a village just outside Jerusalem.

They had heard some of Jesus' friends say that they'd seen Jesus alive again.

But they felt sad, because they still thought Jesus was dead.

Suddenly a stranger appeared and started to walk along the road with them.

It was Jesus – but they didn't recognize him.

"What were you talking about?" Jesus asked the men.
Looking very gloomy, they described
what had been happening in Jerusalem.
They explained that Jesus had died on the cross.

A stranger to supper

By now the men were approaching their village.

"Stay with us," the friends said to Jesus. "It will be dark soon."

So Jesus ate supper with them.

Jesus broke the bread and gave some to each of the men.

At that moment the men saw that the stranger was Jesus!

Then he disappeared.

"That was Jesus!" said one of them.
"Didn't you feel excited when he was talking to us on the road?"
They jumped up and rushed back to Jerusalem.
"It's true!" they told the disciples.
"Jesus *is* alive! We've seen him with our very own eyes!"

Jesus is alive

Forty days later, Jesus' disciples were all together
in a house in Jerusalem.

Suddenly Jesus appeared in the room.

At first they all felt really frightened.

"Don't be afraid," Jesus said calmly.

"Men killed me – but God has brought me back to life.
I want you to go to every country in the world," he said.

"Tell everyone that God loves them.
You shall be my messengers."

Jesus goes away

After this, Jesus walked with his disciples
to the Mount of Olives, just outside Jerusalem.
　　They stood together on the hill.
　　"Now I am going to be with God," Jesus said.
"But I'm still with you. And I always will be."

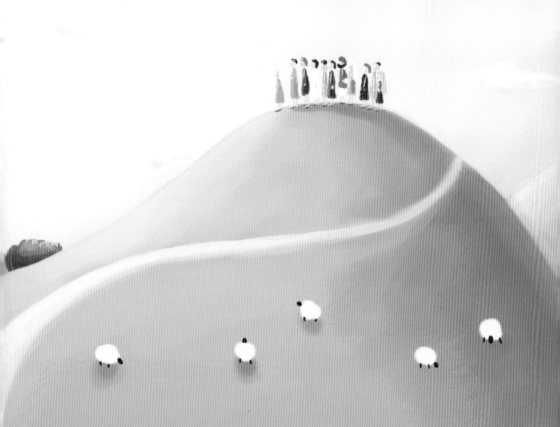

As Jesus was talking, a cloud came down from the sky.
It took Jesus away.

When the cloud disappeared, the disciples couldn't see Jesus.
They stood staring up into the sky, hoping to see Jesus again.

Jesus will return

Suddenly two angels appeared.

"Why are you all staring up at the sky?" asked the angels. "Jesus is now with God in heaven. One day he will return. Now just do as Jesus told you."

So the disciples walked back to Jerusalem very happy.

They went to the Temple to thank God for everything that had happened.

And they began to spread the good news about Jesus.